WHAT IS THIS?

a. the head and torso of an alien secretly recovered by the U.S. military

b. a bald-headed monkey

c. a tourist attraction from a museum in Roswell, New Mexico

C. a tourist attraction from a museum in Roswell, New Mexico

This exhibit at the International UFO Museum and Research Center shows an alien autopsy. A medical worker is examining a dead alien.

Both the medical worker and the alien in this exhibit are dummies. But according to some people, this scene is based on fact. They say an alien spacecraft crashed in Roswell, New Mexico, in 1947. The bodies of the aliens were then taken to an army base nearby — and autopsied.

But did these autopsies ever occur? And did a spacecraft really crash? Read on to find out more.

Book design Red Herring Design/NYC

Library of Congress Cataloging-in-Publication Data
Grace, N. B.
UFOs : what scientists say may shock you! / N. B. Grace.
p. cm. – (24/7: science behind the scenes)
Includes bibliographical references and index.
ISBN-13: 978-0-531-12074-3 (lib. bdg.) 978-0-531-18741-8 (pbk.)
ISBN-10: 0-531-12074-0 (lib. bdg.) 0-531-18741-1 (pbk.)
1. Unidentified flying objects—Sightings and encounters. I. Title.
TL789.3.G675 2008
001.942—dc22   2007043580

UFOs

What Scientists Say May Shock You!

N. B. Grace

Franklin Watts
An Imprint of Scholastic Inc.
New York • Toronto • London • Auckland • Sydney
Mexico City • New Delhi • Hong Kong
Danbury, Connecticut

CONTENTS

Get the 411 on unidentified flying objects.

8

OVERHEARD
Speaking of Aliens . . .

10

SEE FOR YOURSELF
Alien Invasions?

14

WHO'S WHO?
The E.T. Team

RECORD PHONES
Business Office 2288

Record

ures Flying Saucer
in Roswell Region

No Details of
Flying Disk
Are Revealed

Ex-King Carol Weds Mme. Lupescu

Roswell Hardware
Man and Wife
Report Disk Seen

A flying disc makes headlines in New Mexico.

Find out about people who may have made contact with aliens!

17 Case #1:
The Roswell UFO Mystery
Did an alien ship crash to Earth in the New Mexico desert?

Case #2:
The Case of Betty and Barney Hill
27 **Was a New Hampshire couple really abducted by aliens?**

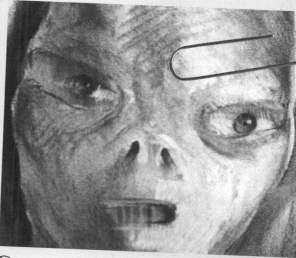

Did an alien like this one abduct a couple from New Hampshire?

35 Case #3:
The "Wow!" Signal
Astronomers pick up a signal from outer space. Could it be a communication from a distant planet?

Did this huge device receive a message from outer space?

Still hoping for a close encounter? Keep reading.

44 FLASHBACK
Key Dates in the History of UFOs

46 RIPPED FROM THE HEADLINES
In the News

48 REAL STUFF
Earth Calling

50 **It Came From Hollywood!**

52 CAREERS
Help Wanted: Astronomer

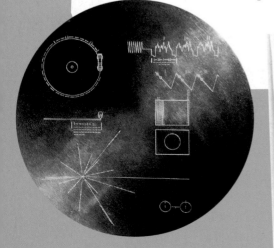

YELLOW PAGES

56 RESOURCES

59 DICTIONARY

62 INDEX

64 AUTHOR'S NOTE

Every year, thousands of people report seeing UFOs. Hundreds more claim they have been kidnapped by aliens. Do all these people have overactive imaginations? Or could it be that we're not alone in the universe?

UFOS 411

These questions have attracted investigators of all kinds—from real scientists to, well, researchers with overactive imaginations.

IN THIS SECTION:

- ▶ how astronomers and UFO researchers really talk;
- ▶ photographs that are not always what they seem;
- ▶ the people who investigate these mysterious cases.

Speaking of Aliens . . .

Some of the terms used in the search for extraterrestrial life may seem a little alien.

> We just got a call from a woman who says she was **abducted** by **aliens**.

abducted
(ub-DUKT-ed) taken away by force

aliens
(AY-lee-uhnz) beings from another planet or another part of the universe

> No, but she says she can describe the **extraterrestrial**.

extraterrestrial
(EK-struh-tur-ess-tree-ul) something that comes from someplace beyond Earth

Extra means "beyond or outside something." Terra means "earth."

Did the case involve a **UFO** sighting, too?

UFO
(yoo-eff-oh) a flying object that cannot be identified or explained; stands for *unidentified flying object*

Make sure she speaks to an **astronomer** or a **ufologist**.

astronomer
(uh-STRAW-nuh-mur) a scientist who studies outer space

ufologist
(yoo-FAH-luh-jist) a professional or amateur researcher who studies UFOs

Say What?

Here's some other lingo a ufologist might use on the job.

car stop
(kar stahp) a UFO encounter in which a witness reports his or her car mysteriously turning off
*"That sighting on the highway in New Mexico involved a **car stop**."*

foo fighter
(foo FYTE-ur) term used by World War II pilots for UFOs
*"I've got a **foo fighter** off my left wing! Request permission to fire."*

grays
(grayz) types of aliens commonly described by supposed witnesses. "Grays" have gray skin, large eyes, and big heads.
*"These days, nearly all aliens on science-fiction shows are **grays**."*

MTE
(em tee ee) stands for *missing time experience*. People who report abduction experiences often feel as though they've blacked out for several hours.
*"It doesn't take two hours to carry out the trash—sounds like an **MTE** to me."*

An army official poses with mysterious debris. Was it the wreckage of a UFO?

WRECKAGE IN ROSWELL

DATE: June 1947

PLACE: Roswell, New Mexico

STORY: A rancher found the wreckage of something bizarre in the middle of the desert. He alerted the nearby Roswell Army Air Field, launching the most famous UFO case of all time. At first, the Air Force said they had found a crashed flying saucer. Later, a general appeared with the debris and claimed the wreckage came from a weather balloon. (See pages 20–21.)

CONTACT?: Probably not. Decades later, the Air Force said they had been testing top-secret balloons for spying on the Russians. One of the balloons crashed near Roswell, and military officers had trouble identifying the high-tech material. But a lot of people still believe Roswell is one of the biggest cover-ups of all time.

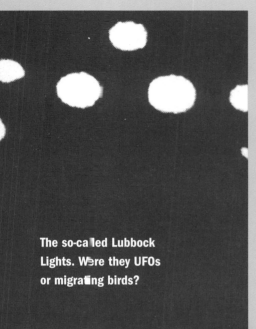

The so-called Lubbock Lights. Were they UFOs or migrating birds?

THE LUBBOCK LIGHTS
DATE: August 31, 1951
PLACE: Lubbock, Texas
STORY: An 18-year-old student took this picture of the so-called Lubbock Lights. Between August and November, at least 100 people saw lights arranged in a crescent shape streaking across the sky. Among the first to observe the lights were three university professors.
CONTACT?: Probably not, but no one has come up with a satisfying explanation. Military officials investigated. They decided that the UFOs were probably migrating birds reflecting the city lights.

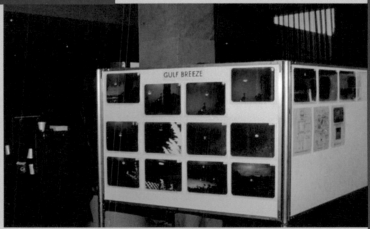

An exhibit of Edward Walters's UFO photos. But were these images fake?

GULF BREEZE

EDWARD WALTERS: ALIEN MAGNET?
DATE: 1987–1990
PLACE: Gulf Breeze, Florida
STORY: A contractor named Edward Walters claimed he was visited repeatedly by aliens. He produced photos that couldn't be proved fake. Over the next three years, more than 200 people in the area claimed to have seen—and in some cases photographed—UFOs.
CONTACT?: Probably not. Walters passed psychiatric tests and two lie detector tests. And the 200 other sightings haven't been explained. But in 1990, Walters sold his house, and the new owner found a small model of a UFO in the attic. Walters never confessed to a hoax. And he got $200,000 for a book on his story and $400,000 for the movie rights.

A REAL ALIEN AUTOPSY?

DATE: August 28, 1995

PLACE: on U.S. TV

STORY: An estimated one billion people watched a show called *Alien Autopsy: Fact or Fiction?* The program was first aired on Fox TV. It featured clips from a film that supposedly showed military doctors operating on alien bodies. A British film producer claimed he had bought the film from a U.S. Army cameraman who had shot it in Roswell, New Mexico, in 1947.

CONTACT?: No. In 2006 a special-effects expert named John Humphreys admitted that he made models out of latex and clay for the film. For the organs, Humphreys used sheep brains and chicken guts from a local meat market.

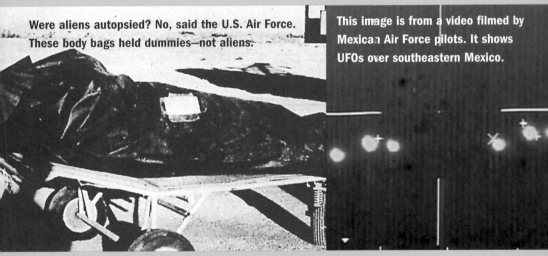

Were aliens autopsied? No, said the U.S. Air Force. These body bags held dummies—not aliens.

This image is from a video filmed by Mexican Air Force pilots. It shows UFOs over southeastern Mexico.

UFOS VERSUS THE MEXICAN AIR FORCE

DATE: March 5, 2007

PLACE: Campeche, Mexico

STORY: Military pilots in the Mexican Air Force filmed UFOs flying over Campeche, a state in southeastern Mexico. The pilots were patrolling for drug smugglers when they were surrounded by bright, darting balls of light. "Was I afraid? Yes. A little afraid because we were facing something that had never happened before," recalled radar operator Lieutenant German Marin. Pilot Magdaleno Castanon said they chased the UFOs. "I believe they could feel we were pursuing them," Castanon said.

CONTACT?: Possibly, but the UFOs weren't discovered until the video footage was reviewed after the flight. And the pilots didn't claim to have chased the lights until after interest in the story had grown. Suggested causes of this UFO sighting have included ball lightning, meteorites, and flares from nearby oil wells.

A FLYING CIGAR?

DATE: March 1987

PLACE: Belleville, Wisconsin

STORY: Between January and March 1987, there were four UFO sightings in the town of Belleville. Some residents there saw objects like this one, shaped like a cylinder. These cylindrical objects supposedly rose up out of forests—in broad daylight.

CONTACT?: There are plenty of eyewitnesses who saw some strange sights. The Illinois Air Traffic Control even reported a UFO in the area. But there's no proof that what people saw was from outer space. The town now hosts a UFO Day every fall.

This is an artist's representation of a UFO sighting in Belleville, Wisconsin.

CLOSE ENCOUNTERS

Some ufologists refer to UFO sightings as "close encounters." According to the terminology, there are four types of close encounters:

Close Encounters of the First Kind: Seeing a UFO from a distance

Close Encounters of the Second Kind: Seeing a UFO that leaves some physical evidence behind (like scorched earth from the engines)

Close Encounters of the Third Kind: Seeing an alien

Close Encounters of the Fourth Kind: Being abducted by aliens. Many UFO researchers are skeptical about whether abductions have ever really happened.

Richard Dreyfuss plays a man who meets peaceful aliens in the 1977 film *Close Encounters of the Third Kind*.

13

The E.T. Team

Professional scientists as well as amateurs have joined the search for extraterrestrial life.

UFOLOGISTS

They are researchers who investigate UFO sightings and close encounter reports. Some are trained scientists. Others have little or no scientific training.

FOLKLORISTS

They study the common beliefs, traditions, and stories of a culture. Some folklorists who study UFOs believe that stories of alien contact are influenced by popular science fiction, fantasy, and other widely known stories.

ENGINEERS

Some engineers build giant radio telescopes that are used to search for extraterrestrial life.

?

PSYCHOLOGISTS

They study how the human mind works. Those who are interested in UFO studies interview people who claim to have had contact with aliens.

ASTRONOMERS

They are scientists who study the universe by observing planets, stars, and galaxies.

ASTROBIOLOGISTS

These scientists study how life began in the universe and the conditions needed for it to survive. Some are searching for life on Mars and several moons in the solar system.

SOCIOLOGISTS

They study how humans interact with each other and the world around them. Some sociologists work to explain mass sightings of UFOs and similar group behaviors.

TRUE-LIFE CASE FILES!

24 hours a day, 7 days a week, 365 days a year, ufologists and other researchers are investigating otherworldly mysteries.

IN THIS SECTION:

▶ a mysterious craft crashes in the New Mexico desert;

▶ a couple claims they were kidnapped by aliens on a New Hampshire highway;

▶ scientists hear a signal from outer space, and no one knows who or what sent it.

Prove It!

Road sign near Roswell, New Mexico.

Plenty of people claim that aliens have visited Earth. But scientists have to ask: Where's the evidence?

The study of UFOs is like a sports rivalry. There are very few neutral parties. Most UFO researchers are either **believers** or **skeptics**. The believers usually set out to prove that we've been contacted by aliens. The skeptics often set out to show that reports of alien encounters are **hoaxes**, **hallucinations**, or mistakes. In the midst of this rivalry, science often gets lost.

What would it take to prove the contact theory scientifically? Scientists require **data**, or **evidence**, to confirm a theory. Evidence of alien contact comes in a few different forms, some more reliable than others.

Eyewitness accounts: Many eyewitnesses are described as sane and level-headed. (U.S. President Jimmy Carter claimed to have seen a UFO.) But even the most reliable witnesses aren't always sure of what they saw.

Photos: Some UFO pictures look remarkably real. But is it really possible to prove that a photo depicts an alien spaceship?

Physical traces: Broken branches and compressed earth have been found at UFO sites. Abductees have claimed that they received alien **implants**. Sometimes, pieces of metal or other objects have been removed from their bodies.

Physical evidence is often reliable. But tests have never shown that any of this evidence came from beyond Earth.

No other explanation: People who believe that aliens have come to Earth often point to the fact that some sightings have never been explained. Does that prove the existence of extraterrestrials? Absolutely not, say the skeptics.

"Unexplained cases are simply unexplained," wrote scientist Hudson Hoagland. "They can never constitute evidence for any **hypothesis**."

Read on. You'll encounter plenty of evidence. Does it constitute proof? That's for you to decide.

Roswell, New Mexico
June 1947

The Roswell UFO Mystery

**Did an alien ship
crash to Earth in the
New Mexico desert?**

The Sighting

A New Mexico rancher finds some suspicious debris in the desert.

After a thunderstorm in 1947, Mac Brazel found strange, shiny wreckage on his ranch. Later, he wondered whether the debris was the remains of a UFO.

On the night of June 13, 1947, a fierce thunderstorm battered the lonely desert around Roswell, New Mexico. The next morning, a ranch foreman named W. W. "Mac" Brazel saddled up his horse and rode out to check for lost sheep.

On his rounds, Brazel came across a field full of strange wreckage. Wandering through the mess, he found odd-looking rubber strips, tinfoil, and sheets of very tough paper. Some of the **debris** had pieces of tape on it with strange flower-like designs.

Brazel was in a hurry at the time and didn't get back to the wreckage for three weeks. He then loaded up some sacks with debris and set off for Roswell. There, he found the newspapers full of strange stories. On June 24, a pilot in Washington State had supposedly seen nine strange craft buzzing past his plane at 1,200 miles per hour (1,931 kph). And dozens of other people came forward with similar tales. Each of them claimed to have seen unexplainable objects in the sky. Reporters started calling the objects "flying saucers" or "flying discs."

Could it be that Brazel had found the remains of a flying saucer? The rancher went straight to the town sheriff with his story. The sheriff knew exactly where to go. Roswell was home to Roswell

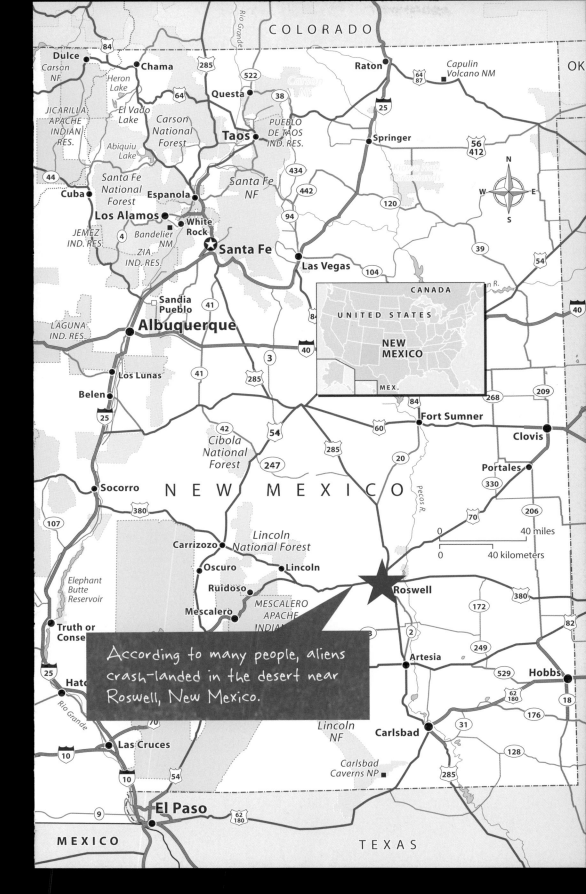

According to many people, aliens crash-landed in the desert near Roswell, New Mexico.

Army Air Field, which was a base for bombers that carried nuclear weapons. On July 7, Brazel and the sheriff called the base The story they told launched the most enduring UFO mystery of all time.

Mystery Solved?

The Air Force offers an explanation—or two.

Major Jesse Marcel, an intelligence officer from Roswell Army Air Field, immediately took up the case. Marcel and another officer met Brazel at the site. Together they dug through the debris. They tried to piece together an object they could recognize.

Marcel gave up after a couple of hours. The debris was too unusual. He collected the material and brought it back to the base. No one there could identify it either.

A colonel at the army base in Roswell sent the wreckage off to the Eighth Army Air Force headquarters in Texas. Then he released a shocking statement. The Air Force, he said, had discovered a "flying disc" from outer space.

The next day, newspapers spread the story around the country. Embarrassed by the news, a general from the Eighth Army Air Force changed the story. He laid out the debris in his Texas office. Then he invited reporters in.

The wreckage, the general said, did not come from a UFO. It was simply the remains of a weather balloon. The reporters left the room satisfied. In the papers the next day, they reported that the "disc" had been explained.

The mystery, it seemed, had been solved. Most people had no reason to doubt the army—until Jesse Marcel spoke out and gave them one.

In 1978, just before he died, Marcel told the *National Enquirer* that the army had lied. The material shown to reporters in 1947, he claimed, was not the material he found in the desert. The debris from the desert had strange qualities, he said. The tinfoil-like substance couldn't be burned with a blowtorch or dented with a sledgehammer. It was, he said, "like nothing made on Earth."

Major Jesse Marcel in 1947, with the debris that was shown to reporters. In 1978, he claimed that this debris was not the material he had found at the crash site.

21

Little Gray Men

Witnesses claim that super-tinfoil wasn't the only thing to fall from the sky near Roswell.

Marcel's revelations reopened the Roswell case. A flood of UFO researchers headed for New Mexico. They found literally hundreds of people who claimed to know something about the crash. And many of these witnesses had a curious story to tell. They insisted that metal and rubber weren't the only things found in the desert in June 1947. Alien bodies had fallen to Earth as well.

A man named Grady L. Barnett said he had found wreckage from a flying saucer near Brazel's ranch. Next to the wreckage lay four small bodies with tiny arms and legs, big heads, and large slanted eyes. Barnett said the military took the bodies away and told him not to talk about what he had seen.

Frank Kaufman had worked at the Roswell Army Air Field in 1947. He claimed that five alien bodies were recovered from the crash. According to Kaufman, the aliens had ash-colored skin, big eyes, fine features, and no hair. "They were very good-looking people," he said.

Witness after witness told stories of alien bodies that were hustled off in great secrecy. Could it be that the U.S. military had found evidence of extraterrestrial life?

Many Roswell researchers believe that the

army had a top-secret lab to study UFOs. The lab was supposedly located in Hangar 18 at the Wright-Patterson Air Force Base near Dayton, Ohio.

Some researchers claim to have evidence that Hangar 18 had been receiving alien remains for years. One ex-army pilot said he saw five crates arrive there in 1953. Each crate supposedly contained a four-foot (1.2-m) body with a large, hairless head packed in dry ice.

A military doctor claimed that he did an autopsy on an alien in the 1950s. His description sounded just like countless others. The alien's head was "pear-shaped" and "oversized." Its eyes had no eyelids. And its nose was little more than a couple of holes in the face.

According to a lieutenant colonel at Wright-Patterson, the Roswell debris was studied in Hangar 18. Most people at the base, he claimed, agreed that the debris had come from outer space.

An army colonel named Philip J. Corso said that the debris made it to his office in Washington 14 years later. He claimed that he turned it over to scientists in private industry, telling them it had come from foreign countries. According to Corso, the debris was then used to create **lasers** and other amazing advances in technology.

Many people believe that evidence from Roswell was stored in Hanger 18 at the Wright-Patterson Air Force Base in Ohio.

The Official Story—Again

Something secretive happened in the desert that summer—but was it a visit from aliens?

In 1994, the Air Force claimed that the debris found near Roswell was the wreckage from a top-secret spy balloon like this one.

After nearly four decades of silence, the Air Force finally did its own research into the Roswell incident. In 1994, it came forward with its explanation of the Roswell mystery. According to the Air Force report, there were no aliens and no autopsies.

The military did admit, however, that something secretive was happening in New Mexico that summer. It was called Project Mogul. During the first week of June 1947, the Air Force had launched four top-secret, high-tech balloons. They were designed to listen for nuclear-bomb tests 10,000 miles (16,090 km) away in the Soviet Union. One of the balloons disappeared after high winds blew it off course.

According to the Air Force, the balloons' parts matched perfectly with the debris found on Brazel's ranch. But the high-tech material was so unusual that no one at the Roswell base recognized it. The report even had an explanation for the flowered tape. It had been made at a toy factory.

But what about the "alien bodies"? The Air Force suggested two explanations. They could have been crash-test dummies dropped from high-altitude balloons. Or they could have been victims of a plane crash in which 11 people burned to death. These events didn't happen

The Air Force claimed that the so-called aliens were actually crash-test dummies (like the figure in the middle), dropped from spy balloons.

until the 1950s. But, as the Air Force pointed out, memories can get a little foggy after 25 years.

True Believers

After 50 years, many people still think Roswell is the world's greatest unsolved mystery.

The military's report about spy balloons and crash-test dummies hasn't convinced a lot of UFO believers. "The only dummies in the whole thing would be us if we believed a word of this," said ufologist Dennis Balthaser.

Many people, like Balthaser, still think that aliens dropped to Earth near Roswell in 1947. Dozens of books have been written arguing that the U.S. military knew what happened and has covered it up for 50 years. If that is true, it is one of the greatest **conspiracies** in modern history.

But if the military told the truth, why did so many people claim to have seen evidence of aliens at Roswell? Were they just looking for attention? Did they convince themselves because they wanted so badly to believe in UFOs?

Or did aliens really crash in the New Mexico desert? **24/7**

PROJECT BLUE BOOK

The Air Force's not-so-secret UFO office decides that most UFOs are not "U" at all.

Many UFO researchers are convinced that the Air Force spent years secretly examining alien remains.

In fact, the military did have an office that investigated UFO claims. Project Blue Book, as it was called, was located at Wright-Patterson Air Force Base in Ohio. But it was hardly secret. It regularly reported to the press on its findings. And its officials never admitted any evidence of aliens. They decided that most unidentified flying objects were easily identifiable.

Between 1952 and 1969, Project Blue Book looked into more than 12,000 UFO reports. In the end, 700 of them remained unsolved. The rest fell into one of four categories.

Conventional objects: Many UFOs turned out to be planes, balloons, or even flocks of birds. The Air Force admitted that some were its own spy planes. Military officials had lied to keep them secret.

Atmospheric or astronomical events: Some kinds of weather, such as ball lightning, look very unusual. Very bright stars and strange-looking clouds have also been labeled UFOs.

Psychological problems: Some UFO sighters were mentally disturbed, the military said. Others were too easily influenced by other UFO sightings.

Hoaxes: A small number of UFO sightings were deliberate pranks.

By 1969, the Air Force was satisfied with its findings. It closed Project Blue Book, saying that it had found no evidence of alien contact.

That didn't silence the critics. Some people say the investigators tried to discredit honest witnesses. After all, the project's main purpose was to calm a fearful public. Others point out that 700 of the cases were never solved!

In this case, the evidence consisted of some strange debris found in the desert. What happens when someone claims to have seen a spaceship — and been taken aboard?

The Case of Betty and Barney Hill

Was a New Hampshire couple really abducted by aliens?

The Encounter

A UFO visits the Hills on a deserted New Hampshire highway.

Betty and Barney Hill had a strange experience on a dark New Hampshire road. They came to believe they'd been abducted by aliens. Here, they're holding a book written about their experiences.

By all accounts, Betty and Barney Hill were a sensible couple. Barney worked for the postal service near their home in Portsmouth, New Hampshire. Betty was a social worker. He was black; she was white. Their interracial marriage was unusual in the 1960s. But they fit in comfortably. Their friends respected them. They were leaders in their community and their church. They were not the kind of people who played pranks or made up wild stories.

Yet Betty and Barney Hill are famous for telling one of the strangest stories ever heard. Every word of their tale has been examined by astronomers, psychologists, and journalists. Almost 50 years later, many people still believe that on September 19, 1961, the Hills were kidnapped by aliens.

That night, Betty and Barney were driving home from vacation in Canada. At about 10:15, they recalled later, a bright light appeared in the sky. Betty thought it was a satellite. Barney decided it was a plane.

But as they kept driving, the light dipped low. It headed for their car. Barney stopped in the middle of the highway and got out. He saw a giant disc hovering 80 to 100 feet (24 to 30 m) above the car. He picked up a pair of binoculars and saw several human-like figures staring at

In September 1961, Betty and Barney Hill were traveling from Quebec to their home in Portsmouth, New Hampshire. What exactly happened that fateful night?

him through a window in the disc. Somehow, Barney claimed, one of the figures sent a message to him: "Stay where you are and keep looking."

Barney obeyed until a ramp began to drop from the bottom of the ship. Then he ran for the car yelling, "They're going to capture us!"

The Hills sped toward home. The disc drifted off. But something felt wrong. The Hills heard a buzzing from the back of the car. They both felt a tingling in their skin and a dull sensation in their heads.

Betty, whose sister claimed to have seen a UFO several years earlier, turned to Barney. "Now do you believe in flying saucers?" she asked.

"Don't be ridiculous," he said.

Missing Time

Three hours disappear from the Hills' memories. Are they coming back in Betty's dreams?

Back at home, the Hills struggled to figure out what had happened. They both felt dirty and took long showers. Betty's dress had been torn and had pink dust on it. She stuffed their clothes in a closet, thinking they had been contaminated with **radiation**.

A day later, Betty reported the event to an Air Force officer. The officer interviewed them and said he would write up a report. But Betty wasn't satisfied. She started reading books on UFOs and contacted one of the authors.

Then Betty's nightmares began. In the dreams, Betty and Barney entered the spaceship. Small bald men with large foreheads led them up the ramp. They separated the couple for medical exams. Betty had her hair clipped and her skin scraped for samples. Someone stabbed her belly with a needle for a pregnancy test.

When the tests were over, Betty talked with her captors. She asked where they came from. The captain of the ship showed her a map of the stars. Then the aliens sent her back to the car.

Betty was convinced that what she saw in her dreams had really happened. In October and November, the Hills had two meetings with UFO researchers. As they told their story, they realized that a few hours were missing from their

Barney Hill shows a drawing of the UFO that he and his wife, Betty, claimed they saw one night in 1961.

accounts. Their car trip that night should have taken four hours; instead it took seven. Was it possible that Betty was recalling the missing hours in her dreams? The researchers suggested that the Hills see a **hypnotist** to help them find out.

Barney's Story

Under hypnosis, a bizarre tale emerges.

It took the Hills two years to get to a hypnotist. Barney refused to believe they had seen a spaceship. But he couldn't come up with an explanation that made sense. In the spring of 1962, the Hills drove the route again and again, trying to remember what had happened. Barney was feeling stress from the mystery. He had an ulcer and his blood pressure was high. That summer, they began to see a **psychiatrist**.

Finally, in December 1963, the Hills went to see Dr. Benjamin Simon in Boston. Simon was a **psychologist** who specialized in hypnosis. Over the next six months, the Hills saw Simon several times. The doctor put them into trance-like states.

Dr. Benjamin Simon (*left*) hypnotized Betty and Barney Hill to help them remember the details of their possible abduction.

Then he asked them questions about the mysterious night of September 19, 1961.

Under hypnosis, Betty repeated the story from her dreams. She also drew, as best she could, the star map she had supposedly seen on the spaceship.

Barney told a story that sounded much like Betty's. On September 19, he said, he was taken aboard the spaceship. He was met by small aliens, like the ones in Betty's dreams. They had large, intense eyes that wrapped around the sides of their heads. Like Betty, Barney had a medical exam. Then he was led back to his car.

This image of an alien was based on descriptions that the Hills offered under hypnosis.

Under hypnosis, Barney often got angry; sometimes he cried. The memories seemed real and painful. By the summer, he was convinced that he and Betty had been kidnapped by aliens.

Dr. Simon was not so sure. He was amazed by how strongly the experience had affected the Hills. He was convinced they were not consciously inventing the story. But he suspected that Barney was influenced by Betty's dreams. It could be, he concluded, that they misunderstood an event they couldn't explain.

Mystery Men

Experts try to explain what happened to the Hills that September night.

After the hypnosis sessions, the Hills tried to remain private. But in October 1965, a reporter uncovered their story. His article ran in the *Boston Traveler* under the headline: "UFO Chiller: Did THEY Seize Couple?"

Since then, many people have asked the same question. No one has come up with a satisfying answer. Nearly everyone who met the Hills agreed that they were mentally stable.

Many people think the story came from Betty's dreams. Under hypnosis, they say, Barney simply remembered discussions about the dreams. One skeptic pointed out that a science-fiction show called *The Outer Limits* was on TV 12 days before Barney's first hypnosis session. The show had an alien on it with wraparound eyes. Barney could have gotten his description of the aliens from the show.

In the end, there was no physical evidence of the kidnapping. Pieces of Betty's dress were tested several times. Nothing unusual was found. Her star map was examined by astronomers. Some claimed to recognize patterns from the actual sky. Others insisted the map was just random dots.

Whatever the truth of their story, it made the Hills famous. Barney died in 1969. Betty lived another 35 years. Over the years, she claimed to have seen several more UFOs. **24/7**

In 2000, Betty Hill (*center*) stood at the spot where she said she was abducted. Over the years, she claimed to have seen more UFOs.

KIDNAPPED?
Could thousands of people all be wrong?

Betty and Barney Hill were among the first to go public with an alien abduction story. But they're not the only ones. Thousands of people claim to have been kidnapped by aliens.

These stories often follow the same pattern. People are taken aboard a spaceship, usually by small, gray-skinned creatures with large heads. The aliens perform a medical exam, during which many people report feeling paralyzed. Then the aliens release their captives, who have little memory of the event—until it's recovered during hypnosis.

The stories are eerily similar and sincerely told. But are they true?

Sleep Paralysis

Many psychologists say they're not true. They believe that most abduction "memories" are created by **sleep paralysis**. Sixty percent of people experience sleep paralysis at some point. It's a state in which the mind is awake but the body remains asleep, as if paralyzed. People often have hallucinations and see bright lights. Many feel as though they're being watched.

How do these hallucinations get translated into alien abductions? According to one study, some people are simply more open to fantasy than others. Often, critics say, hypnotists help them along by suggesting memories to them.

High-Tech Abductions

Why, then, are the stories so similar? Skeptics say that people pick up signals from science-fiction books and movies. The details in abduction stories, it seems, have changed over the years to follow technological progress on Earth. 'n the Hills' era, the so-called aliens had large machines with flashing lights and whirring dials. Today they tend to use lasers and **holograms**.

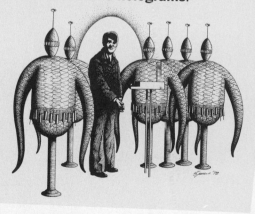

In 1977, a bus driver in Brazil claimed that he was taken aboard a UFO by robot-like aliens. This is an artist's depiction of that abduction.

Columbus, Ohio
August 15, 1977,
11:16 P.M.

The "Wow!" Signal

Astronomers pick up a signal
from outer space. Could it be
a communication from a
distant planet?

A Message From Outer Space?

A computer printout shows an unusual signal from outer space.

For three decades, astronomers from Ohio State University searched the sky using a giant radio telescope known as "Big Ear." Unlike optical telescopes, which are used to look at objects in space, radio telescopes are used to collect radio waves. Those radio waves come from sources such as stars and provide lots of information for scientists. But Big Ear was also "listening" for something else—a message from aliens.

On August 15, 1977, Big Ear was pointed toward the constellation Sagittarius. All day, the usual weak "noise" came in—radio static from deep space, satellites, and sources on Earth. Then, Big Ear picked up a sudden burst. The signal lasted for 72 seconds. It was recorded on a paper printout. Then it was gone.

Big Ear was as big as three football fields. At one end it had a giant metal panel tilted towards the sky so it could pick up radio signals from stars and planets—and maybe from aliens. In 1998, Big Ear was demolished to make room for a golf course.

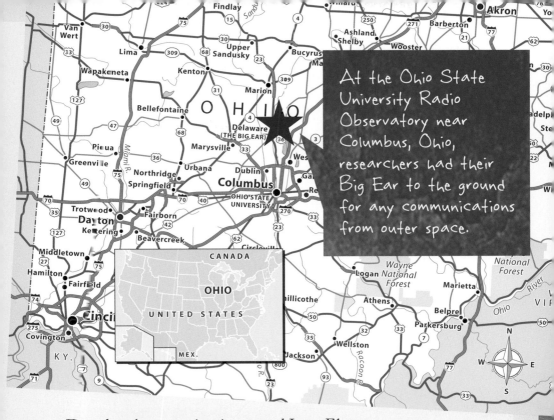

At the Ohio State University Radio Observatory near Columbus, Ohio, researchers had their Big Ear to the ground for any communications from outer space.

Four days later, a scientist named Jerry Ehman examined Big Ear's printout. The signal didn't look like much. It was just a series of numbers and letters printed vertically on a page full of numbers: "6EQUJ5." But Ehman had never seen anything like it. Big Ear recorded signals every 12 seconds, and computers turned them into a code of letters and numbers. The weaker signals got numbers, from 1 to 10. Stronger signals got letters, from A to Z. Rarely did Big Ear pick up a signal stronger than a 4. But here was a pulse that went all the way to U!

Ehman was amazed. He scribbled the word "Wow!" on the computer printout next to the recorded signal.

Could it have been the very first message from aliens to Earth?

Listen Carefully

Many scientists think there must be life out there somewhere.

A printout of the famous "Wow!" signal. The scientist Jerry Ehman circled the letters and numbers that represented a stronger radio pulse than had ever been heard from deep space.

Big Ear had been scanning the skies for 14 years when it picked up the so-called "Wow!" signal. Its search was inspired by the work of an astronomer named Frank Drake.

In 1961, Drake came up with a theory based on some relatively simple math. He knew there were roughly 100 billion stars in our Milky Way galaxy. He estimated how many of those stars might have planets similar to Earth. With a few more calculations, he decided there could be 10,000 planets in our galaxy alone that support intelligent life.

Drake's theory couldn't be tested.

But suppose it were true: There could easily be creatures out there trying to communicate with us. Drake decided that human beings should be listening. So, he started a research effort known as SETI: the Search for Extraterrestrial Intelligence.

From the start, SETI had two big obstacles. First, the universe is huge. Second, radio telescopes can't search the entire sky. They have to focus on one area at a time.

Then, even if SETI scientists pick the right spot, they still have to pick the right channel. Radio waves travel at different **frequencies**. To listen to a **transmission**, a receiver has to be tuned to the same frequency as the sender. When you choose a station on your radio, you're tuning in to its frequency.

Astronomers selected a frequency for Big Ear to listen to—1,420 gigahertz. They pointed the panel in one direction at a time and used Earth's rotation to sweep the sky. Now, after 14 years, had they suddenly gotten lucky?

Signing Off

Scientists try to explain the signal—or at least find it again.

Ehman and others studied the "Wow!" printout. One fact made them think they may have heard from a distant civilization. The signal lasted 72 seconds. That's exactly the amount of time it took for Big Ear's beam to sweep a single spot in the sky. The beam was most sensitive at its center. Therefore, a signal from a fixed point in space would start weakly, gain in strength, then fall as the beam passed over it. That was exactly the pattern followed by the "Wow!" signal.

This observation seemed to rule out a lot of sources for the signal. A source on Earth would have bypassed the beam, flooding the telescope directly. It would have started at full strength, then ended abruptly. The timing of the signal also seemed to rule out moving sources. A signal from a plane or an orbiting satellite would not have lasted exactly 72 seconds.

But Big Ear's astronomers were stumped by another important detail. After one observation, the "Wow!" signal completely disappeared. Big Ear had a second beam sweeping the sky three minutes after the first. It picked up nothing. For 30 days, scientists kept Big Ear pointed to the same spot in the sky. They still had no luck.

Since 1977, several major studies have searched for a repeat of the "Wow!" signal. They've all come up empty-handed.

Without a repeat performance, it's impossible to say what caused the signal. It may have been a one-time transmission from an alien world. But as Ehman says, "There's simply too little data to draw many conclusions."

Jill Tarter and Seth Shostak are astronomers who work at the SETI Institute. They search for evidence of alien life in the universe.

Needle in a Haystack

Despite the odds, scientists keep searching for extraterrestrial life.

Despite their failure to find another "Wow!" signal, scientists have not stopped listening. SETI has even gotten ordinary computer users involved. Its SETI@home software allows people around the world to analyze radio data from space. Over three million computer-users in 200 countries participate in the program.

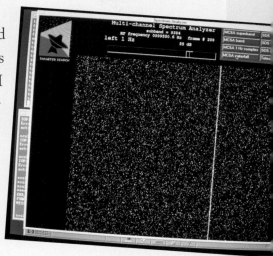

This is an image of a test signal sent out by the SETI Institute. Will alien life pick up a signal like this one and try to communicate?

How likely is it that one of those three million people will find a message from E.T.? A few numbers might help answer the question. Our galaxy is 100,000 **light-years** across. (A light-year is the distance light travels in a year, or about six trillion miles—10 trillion km.) In that vast space, there are more than 100,000 billion stars.

For a message to get through, we would have to get incredibly lucky. First, we would have to pick the right spot in space to listen to. Second, the broadcast would have to be aimed directly at Earth. Third, we would have to be listening to the right frequency.

And finally, the whole effort relies on the assumption that radio waves are the right way to listen. An advanced civilization might have

This is a screen display of the SETI@home software. Computers all over the world use this software to analyze radio data from outer space.

communications technology that we can't even imagine.

Scientists are trying to narrow the search by finding Earth-like planets outside our solar system. Because these planets are too far away to see with even the best telescopes, scientists search for stars that "wobble" because of the pull of planets circling around them. Scientists have found more than 200 planets this way, but almost all of them are too big and too hot to support life. In 2007, astronomers found a planet that is only seven times bigger than Earth. But it's too cold to have liquid water. There are probably no good candidates within 300 light-years.

Suppose we got lucky enough to receive a message from that distance. Radio waves travel at the speed of light, so the message would be 300 years old. Who knows what the civilization would look like by now? Three hundred years ago on Earth, no one had heard of the steam engine, and messages were sent on horseback.

Still, many people think the search is worth the money. After all, if a real message arrives from outer space, "Wow!" would be an understatement. 24/7

UFOS DOWNLOAD

Want to look beyond? Here's more information about the search for alien life.

IN THIS SECTION:

► UFOs in the past;

► otherwordly events in the news;

► a special message for extraterrestrials;

► aliens invade the movie theater;

► astronomy: the career for you?

Key Dates in the History of UFOs

People have been seeing strange things in the sky for thousands of years. Here are a few of the most famous sightings from the past.

Long Ago and Far Away
UFOs in Ancient Egypt

UFO reports existed long before Roswell. In the 15th century B.C., an Egyptian wrote about a fire-circle in the air. The ancient Romans saw "altars in the sky," "gleaming beams," and "night suns." A 12th-century French writer described "a great star like a torch" that took off in a shower of sparks. Evidence of alien contact? Most ufologists say no way. You can't investigate a 2,000-year-old sighting.

November 1896—May 1897
Airships Invade North America

Thousands of people report seeing giant airships. One of them is said to have lassoed a cow in Kansas and airlifted it away. Another supposedly crashes in Texas, killing its pilot. According to the *Dallas Morning News*, the pilot "was not an inhabitant of this world." Historians say many of the sightings were invented by journalists to sell newspapers.

June 24, 1947
Attack of the Flying Saucers

A civilan pilot named Kenneth Arnold sees nine disc-shaped objects flying in formation in Washington. His story starts a wave of sightings that includes the Roswell incident. Newspapers start referring to the objects as "flying saucers." The U.S. military soon launches Project Blue Book to investigate the sightings. In the early 1950s, its director invents the term "UFO."

See page 26.

October 16, 1957 Aliens Abduct Farmer

A Brazilian farmer named Antonio Villas Boas claims he was visited by an egg-shaped spaceship. Aliens in gray suits supposedly took him on board and performed medical experiments on him. Some people think Boas is the first believable victim of an alien abduction. His story is widely publicized four years later, after Betty and Barney Hill claim to have been abducted in New Hampshire.

2006 Believe It or Not!

The latest poll on the subject, from Baylor University, shows that 25 percent of Americans believe that alien spaceships have visited Earth. Some polls place the number as high as 50 percent. Several surveys have suggested that more than two-thirds of Americans think the government is covering up UFO information.

In the News

Search for Earth Nears the End

VANCOUVER, CANADA—May 31, 2007

The search for planet Earth is drawing to a close, as the hit science-fiction series *Battlestar Galactica* enters its final season this year.

The show debuted on the Sci Fi Channel in 2004. It tells the story of the last surviving humans from the Twelve Colonies of Man. When the series began, the human race had nearly been destroyed in a nuclear war with the dreaded Cylons.

The survivors fled in an old fleet of spaceships with the Cylons chasing them. Their only hope is to find the fabled thirteenth colony. It's a planet they know only from ancient religious texts, and its name is Earth.

Battlestar Galactica is the latest in a long line of movies and TV shows in which humans battle aliens in space. The list includes two of the most successful entertainment franchises of all time: *Star Trek* and *Star Wars*.

The cast from the third season of *Battlestar Galactica*.

Area 51 Snoop in the Clear

GROOM LAKE, NEVADA—January 2005

The secrets of Area 51 are safe for now. An amateur astronomer named Chuck Clark has agreed to a year's probation for tampering with a security system at the mysterious military base.

Clark has been watching Area 51 for years. Supposedly the base tests top-secret military aircraft. But UFO enthusiasts think it has an even more secretive purpose. They claim that Area 51 is devoted to the study of aliens and alien technology secretly recovered by the military.

In 2003, Clark discovered a network of motion sensors buried in the ground around the base. Many of them were located on public land used by hikers. Clark dug up 40 of the sensors, examined them, and reburied them. The government charged him with a felony.

Above: A satellite photo of Area 51, a top-secret military base in Groom Lake, Nevada. **Right:** Signs at the entrance of Area 51 warn curious passersby to keep out. The U.S. government used to deny this military base existed, and the base still does not appear on its official maps.

Earth Calling

Thirty years ago, scientists from the U.S. sent their own message into outer space.

In 1977, NASA launched the two *Voyager* spacecraft. Each carried an identical 12-inch gold-plated phonograph record. On each record are a series of sounds and coded images meant to show the "diversity of life and culture on Earth" to extraterrestrials. The surface of the record has instructions for listening to the sounds and decoding the images.

Will aliens ever receive this greeting? Not any time soon. Since leaving our solar system, the *Voyagers* have been drifting through empty space. They won't approach another star for at least 40,000 years.

This shows the record with the needle in the right place to play the record from the beginning. The lines around the disc are meant to explain how fast to spin the record.

This is a side view of the record and needle. The lines represent numbers that tell how long it takes to play one side.

This is a map that shows the location of our solar system.

48

These drawings show how to turn the coded signals on the record into pictures.

This is a copy of the first picture on the record. It is meant to be compared to the first decoded image to show that the decoding is being done correctly.

The cover is coated with uranium-238. Uranium decays at a steady rate. This makes it a kind of radioactive clock. A smart extraterrestrial could use the U-238 to figure out how long the spacecraft has been traveling from Earth.

The images on the record include: the planets of our solar system, male and female bodies, leaves, snowflakes, trees, seashells, dolphins, a gymnast, sprinters, a supermarket, the Taj Mahal (a building in India), the Sydney Opera House (in Australia), rush-hour traffic, and an astronaut in space.

The sound portion of the record includes: surf, wind, thunder, bird and whale calls, music from different cultures and time periods, greetings in 55 languages, and greetings from then-President Jimmy Carter and the Secretary-General of the United Nations.

It Came From Hollywood!

Aliens have been stars ever since the movies began.

One of the first movies ever made had aliens in it. Called *A Trip to the Moon*, it was made in 1902. Since then, many popular movies have featured aliens and space travel. These movies have given us an image of what extraterrestrials might look like (pretty weird) and how they might behave (badly, for the most part).

MONSTROUS OR HUMAN-LIKE?

The big-headed beings in *Invasion of the Saucer-Men* (1957) and *Mars Attacks!* (1996) are typical of how Hollywood has portrayed aliens.

Not all movie aliens have huge heads. Some, like those in *The Man from Planet X* (1951) and *The Brother From Another Planet* (1985), look a lot like humans.

50

NASTY INVADERS . . .

The aliens in *Earth vs. the Flying Saucers* (1956) destroy most of Washington, D.C., before they are defeated.

The attackers in *Strange Invaders* (1983) take over the bodies of people in a small midwestern town.

In *War of the Worlds* (2005), invaders in giant machines try to wipe out all mankind.

. . . OR FRIENDLY BEINGS?

In *Close Encounters of the Third Kind* (1977), a giant UFO (below) arrives on Earth. The aliens on it have come to make friends with humans, not to destroy them.

In *E.T.* (1982), a cute alien (above) is stranded on Earth. The little guy doesn't want to hurt anyone—he just wants to go home.

HELP WANTED:
Astronomer

Can you envision yourself as an astronomer? Here's more information about the field:

Q&A: DR. SETH SHOSTAK

Dr. Seth Shostak is a senior astronomer at the SETI Institute. He also does a weekly podcast called "Are We Alone?" You can listen to it at www.seti.org/radio

24/7: How did you get interested in SETI research?

DR. SETH SHOSTAK: I've liked astronomy since I was eight. I built a telescope when I was ten. In middle school, I became interested in aliens. Then I studied physics in college. I switched to astronomy in graduate school because it seemed more romantic. I was studying galaxies with radio telescopes. It dawned on me that the telescopes could be used to see whether there really are aliens.

24/7: The radio telescope scans for non-visible signals. Do you ever look through a regular telescope?

DR. SHOSTAK: Only amateur astronomers look through [light] telescopes anymore. Your eyes are great for some things but not for seeing faint objects. And you don't even have to be at the radio telescope to check for signals. The computer does that and sends the data to your desktop computer.

24/7: Have you ever thought you had received a signal from aliens?

DR. SHOSTAK: One time we accidentally picked up a signal from a satellite. It looked like it might be an E.T. But on that day, some of our equipment wasn't working. It took most of a day to figure it out.

That's when we found out what will happen if we ever *do* get an alien signal. The word leaked out, and we started getting calls from reporters right away.

24/7: How has SETI research changed during your career?

DR. SHOSTAK: The equipment is not just millions, not just billions, not just trillions, but hundreds of trillions times faster and more sensitive. We also know more than we did in 1960 when the first SETI experiment was planned. We thought there *might* be planets around other stars, but now we *know* there are. That makes us smarter about where to point our telescopes.

24/7: Is there anything else you'd like readers to know about SETI research?

DR. SHOSTAK: It's hard to travel between the stars because the distances are so great. But it's very easy to send messages between the stars. We can do it, and we only invented radio a hundred years ago. So beings on other planets probably can do it, too. This is a special time in human history because we could actually find intelligent life elsewhere in the universe.

THE STATS

JOBS
professor: Many universities have astronomy and astrophysics departments.
consultant in private industry: Private aerospace companies need astronomers to help design satellites, rockets, and other space systems.
researcher at national institutions: Astronomers at organizations like NASA explore new technology and help plan space missions.
planetarium or science museum directors: People with astronomy degrees can also educate the public about outer space.
science writers: Lots of people want to know more about the universe and the exciting new discoveries astronomers are making. An astronomer with good communication skills would make a good reporter for newspapers, magazines, or science journals.

EDUCATION Astronomers must finish the following:
4 years of college;
5–6 years of graduate school for a PhD;
2–3 years at a university in a postdoctoral position to focus on research.

CONTINUED ON PAGE 55

DO YOU HAVE WHAT IT TAKES?

Take this totally unscientific quiz to find out whether astronomy might be a good career for you.

1 **Do you enjoy solving difficult problems?**

a) Yes, I enjoy the challenge.

b) Sometimes I like to take on tough problems.

c) I only think about what's on TV.

2 **Do you have a good imagination?**

a) Yes, I have dozens of ideas every day.

b) Sometimes I have new ideas, but not often.

c) I almost never think of new ideas.

3 **How good are you at sticking with a problem until you solve it?**

a) Very good. I never give up!

b) I'll keep trying for a while, but then I'll give up.

c) I want to find a solution right away so I can move on to something else.

4 **How well do you communicate with others?**

a) I'm very good at writing papers and giving presentations.

b) I need to work on becoming a better writer and speaker.

c) RU KDG? LOL!

5 **How good are you at making observations?**

a) I notice everything around me and pick up on lots of details.

b) I pay attention, but I miss some details.

c) I'm too much of a space cadet to notice what's going on around me!

YOUR SCORE

Give yourself 3 points for every "**a**" you chose. Give yourself 2 points for every "**b**" you chose. Give yourself 1 point for every "**c**" you chose.

If you got **13–15 points**, you'd probably be a good astronomer.

If you got **10–12 points**, you might be a good astronomer.

If you got **5–9 points**, you might want to look at another career!

HOW TO GET STARTED...NOW!

It's never too early to start working toward your goals.

GET AN EDUCATION!

▶ Take as many math and science courses as you can. Also take courses in photography, computer science, and environmental studies.

▶ Start thinking about college. Look for schools that have good astronomy, engineering, physics, computer science, and mathematics departments.

▶ Graduate from high school!

STAY INFORMED

▶ Read the newspaper and visit news sites online. Satellites and UFOs of all kinds are often in the headlines. Keep up with what's going on in science and technology.

▶ Go to the library and get books about satellites, astronomy, the space program, computers, and photography.

▶ There are many great Web sites about space, satellites, and UFOs. Check out the NASA, SPACE.com, NRO, and SETI sites.

▶ Take a look at the books and Web sites listed in the Resources section on pages 56–58.

GET AN INTERNSHIP

▶ Look for an internship at an observatory, with an engineering group, at your local air and space museum, or even at a photography studio. If you live near a NASA facility or near the SETI Institute, try to go on a tour. Ask lots of questions.

▶ You can also get involved in your high school science group, state junior academies of science, and even a local astronomy club.

LEARN ABOUT OTHER JOBS IN THE FIELD

There are lots of jobs out there if you're interested in searching for intelligent life in the universe. For example, SETI employs:

▶ astronomers
▶ biologists
▶ computer scientists
▶ electrical engineers
▶ engineers
▶ linguists
▶ physicists

THE STATS
CONTINUED

MONEY At a university, new assistant professors earn about $50,000.
Senior professors earn between $80,000 to 100,000.
Astronomers can also work for national institutions, such as NASA, or private aerospace companies. These jobs usually pay more than university jobs.

THE NUMBERS
There are about 6,000 professional astronomers in North America.

55

Resources

PROFESSIONAL ORGANIZATIONS

J. Allen Hynek Center for UFO Studies (CUFOS)

www.cufos.org
2457 W. Peterson
Chicago, IL 60659
PHONE: 773-271-3611

This group of international scientists, investigators, professors, and volunteers is dedicated to the examination and analysis of UFO information. CUFOS promotes serious scientific study and provides an archive of reports, publications, and other documents.

National Academy of Sciences (NAS)

www.nasonline.org
500 Fifth Street, NW
Washington, DC 20001
PHONE: 202-334-2000

The NAS is a society of distinguished scholars who do scientific and engineering research. The group is dedicated to furthering progress in science and technology and their use for the benefit of humankind.

National Aeronautics and Space Administration (NASA)

www.nasa.gov
Suite 5K39
Washington, DC 20546-0001
PHONE: 202-358-0001
E-MAIL: public-inquiries@hq.nasa.gov

The mission of this organization is to pioneer the future of exploration and research of outer space. The headquarters of NASA are located in Washington, D.C., but the agency has offices in Florida, Texas, and many other states.

National Reconnaissance Office (NRO)

www.nro.gov
Office of Corporate Communications
14675 Lee Road
Chantilly, VA 20151-1715
PHONE: 703-808-1198

The NRO designs, builds, and operates U.S. government satellites that monitor Earth and its atmosphere. It is staffed by members of the Department of Defense and the Central Intelligence Agency.

WEB SITES

Planetary Society
www.planetary.org
65 North Catalina Avenue
Pasadena, CA 91106
PHONE: 626-793-5100

This is the world's largest space-interest group. It is dedicated to inspiring the public with the adventure and mystery of space exploration.

SETI Institute
www.seti.org
515 N. Whisman Road
Mountain View, CA 94043
PHONE: 650-961-6633

This nonprofit organization is dedicated to scientific research, education, and public outreach. The group's mission is to explore, understand, and explain the origin and nature of life in the universe.

Carl Sagan Center for the Study of Life in the Universe
www.seti.org/csc/index.php

This center, part of the SETI Institute, brings astrobiologists together to study how life began and how it has evolved.

Frank Drake Interview
http://contact-themovie.warner bros.com/cmp/int-drake.html

Read about Dr. Drake's work and his theories about life in the universe.

KidsAstronomy.com
www.kidsastronomy.com

This site provides games, activities, fun facts, and much more.

National UFO Reporting Center
www.ufocenter.com

At this site, users can report UFO sightings or read about UFO history and interesting recent sightings.

SPACE.com
www.space.com

This site offers information about the history of spaceflight, current missions, and what the future may hold.

UFO Casebook
www.ufocasebook.com

On this site, you can view photos and read about reported sightings.

UFO Evidence
www.ufoevidence.org

This site is one of the Internet's largest sources of UFO research and information. It includes more than 2,000 articles, photos, documents, and other resources.

UFO Skeptic
www.ufoskeptic.org

This site offers information for scientists on UFOs.

Voyager Golden Record
http://voyager.jpl.nasa.gov/space craft/goldenrec.html

You can hear the sounds and see many of the images that were sent into outer space as a message to any extraterrestrials who might find it.

BOOKS

Firestone, Mary. *SETI Scientist* (Weird Careers in Science). Broomall, Pa.: Chelsea House, 2005.

Herbst, Judith. *Aliens* (The Unexplained). Minneapolis: Lerner, 2004.

Jackson, Ellen. *Looking for Life in the Universe: The Search for Extraterrestrial Intelligence* (Scientists in the Field). New York: Houghton Mifflin, 2005.

Jeffrey, Gary. *UFOs: Alien Abduction and Close Encounters* (Jr. Graphic Mysteries). New York: Rosen Central, 2006.

Mason, Paul. *Investigating UFOs* (Forensic Files). Chicago: Heinemann, 2004.

Nobleman, Marc Tyler. *Aliens and UFOs* (Atomic). Austin: Raintree, 2006.

Ride, Sally, and Tam O'Shaughnessy. *Exploring Our Solar System.* New York: Crown Books for Young Readers, 2003.

Roleff, Tamara L. *Alien Abductions* (Fact or Fiction?). Chicago: Greenhaven Press, 2003.

Skurzynski, Gloria. *Are We Alone? Scientists Search for Life in Space.* Washington, D.C.: National Geographic Children's Books, 2004.

Southwell, David, and Sean Twist. *Unsolved Extraterrestrial Mysteries* (Mysteries and Conspiracies). New York: Rosen Central, 2007.

A

abducted (ub-DUKT-ed) *verb* taken away by force

aliens (AY-lee-uhnz) *noun* beings from another planet or another part of the universe

astrobiologists (as-troh-bye-AHL-uh-jists) *noun* scientists who study life in the universe and how it began

astronomer (uh-STRAW-nuh-mur) *noun* a scientist who studies the universe by observing planets, stars, and galaxies

B

believers (bee-LEE-vurz) *noun* people who accept certain ideas and theories

C

car stop (kar stahp) *noun* a UFO encounter in which a witness reports his or her car mysteriously turning off

conspiracies (kun-SPEER-uh-seez) *noun* secret plots or schemes

D

data (DAY-tuh) *noun* factual information such as statistics and measurements

debris (deh-BREE) *noun* pieces of something that has been destroyed

E

engineers (en-juh-NEERZ) *noun* people, trained in science and mathematics, who solve practical problems

evidence (EV-uh-duhnss) *noun* information and objects that help people make judgments or come to conclusions

extraterrestrial (EK-struh-tur-ess-tree-ul) *noun* a being that comes from someplace beyond Earth

F

folklorists (FOHK-lor-ists) *noun* people who study the common beliefs, traditions, and stories of a culture

foo fighter (foo FYTE-ur) *noun* term used by Word War II pilots for UFOs

frequencies (FREE-qwen-seez) *noun* the range in which radio waves are transmitted

G

grays (grayz) *noun* a type of alien commonly described by supposed witnesses

H

hallucinations (huh-loo-sih-NAY-shunz) *noun* visual images of things that are not physically there

hoaxes (HOHX-ez) *noun* elaborate tricks

holograms (HOH-luh-gramz) *noun* three-dimensional images produced by beams of light

hypnotist (HIP-nuh-tist) *noun* a person who uses hypnosis to put people into a trance-like state

hypothesis (hye-POTH-uh-sus) *noun* an educated guess or prediction

I

implants (IM-plants) *noun* materials that are inserted in human tissue, such as tracking devices

L

lasers (LAY-zurz) *noun* devices that make very narrow, powerful beams of light, used for surgery, light shows, etc.

light-years (LYTE-yeerz) *noun* measurements of very long distances, each equal to about six trillion miles, or the distance that light travels in one year

M

MTE (em-tee-ee) *noun* stands for *missing time experience.* People who report abduction experiences often feel as though they've blacked out for several hours.

P

psychiatrist (sye-KYE-uh-trist) *noun* a doctor who specializes in treating people with mental or emotional disorders

psychologists (sye-KOL-uh-jists) *noun* professionals who investigate the human mind

R

radiation (ray-dee-AY-shun) *noun* energy given off by radioactive materials; radiation can cause cells in the human body to be destroyed

S

satellite (SAT-uh-lyte) *noun* a spacecraft that orbits Earth or other bodies in space. Some satellites transmit TV signals and others monitor activity on Earth.

skeptics (SKEP-tiks) *noun* people who doubt or question ideas or beliefs

sleep paralysis (sleep puh-RAH-luh-sis) *noun* a state in which the mind is awake but the body is paralyzed, or can't move

sociologists (soh-see-AHL-uh-jists) *noun* professionals who study how humans interact with one another and the world around them

T

transmission (tranz-MISH-un) *noun* a signal or message sent from one place to another

U

UFO (yoo-eff-oh) *noun* a flying object that cannot be identified or explained; stands for *unidentified flying object*

ufologist (yoo-FAH-luh-jist) *noun* a professional or amateur researcher who studies UFOs

It's UFO Time!

Most UFO sightings in the United States take place in the month of July. Most UFOs are seen around 9 P.M. or 3 A.M.

Most UFO sightings in the U.S. are reported in the northeast and the southwest.

Index

abductions, 8, 13, 16, 28–29, 30–31, 32, 33, *33*, 34, *34*, 45
Alien Autopsy: Fact or Fiction? (television show), 12, *12*
aliens, 8, *12*, 13, 22, 23, 24, 25, 26, *32*, 33, 34, *34*, 45, *45*, 47
Area 51, 47, *47*
Arnold, Kenneth, 45
astrobiologists, 14
astronomers, 9, 14, 28, 33, 36, 38, 40, *40*, 42, 47, 52–53, 55
astronomical events, 26
atmospheric events, 26
autopsies, 23, 24

Balthaser, Dennis, 25
Barnett, Grady L., 22
Battlestar Galactica (television show), 46, *46*
Baylor University, 45
Belleville, Wisconsin, 13, *13*
"Big Ear" radio telescope, 36–37, *36*, 38, 39–40
Boas, Antonio Villas, 45
Boston Traveler newspaper, 33
Brazel, W. W. "Mac," 18, *18*, 24
The Brother From Another Planet (movie), *50*

car stops, 9
Carter, Jimmy, 16, 49
Castanon, Magdaleno, 12
Clark, Chuck, 47
close encounters, 13
Close Encounters of the Third Kind (movie), *13*, *51*
conventional objects, 26
Corso, Philip J., 23

Dallas Morning News, 44
Drake, Frank, 38

Dreyfuss, Richard, *13*

Earth vs. the Flying Saucers (movie), *51*
education, 52, 53, 55
Egypt, 44
Ehman, Jerry, 37
Eighth Army Air Force, 20, 21
engineers, 12, 14, 55
E.T. (movie), *51*
evidence, 13, 16, 18, *20*, 21, *21*, 22, 23, *23*, 24, *24*, 25, 26, 33
extraterrestrials, 8, 16, 22, 48, 49, 50
eyewitnesses, 9, 13, 16, 22, 26

folklorists, 14
foo fighters, 9
France, 44

gold record, 48–49, *48–49*
grays, 9, 34
Groom Lake, Nevada, *47*
Gulf Breeze, Florida, 11

Hangar 18, 23, *23*
Hill, Barney, 28–29, *28*, 30, *30*, 31–32, *31*, 33, 34, 45
Hill, Betty, 28–29, *28*, 30–31, *30*, *31*, 31–32, 33, *33*, 34, 45
Hoagland, Hudson, 16
hoaxes, 16, 26
Humphreys, John, 12
hypnosis, 31–32, *31*, *32*, 33

Illinois Air Traffic Control, 13
implants, 16
internships, 55

Kaufman, Frank, 22

Lubbock Lights, 11, *11*
Lubbock, Texas, 11, *11*

Marcel, Jesse, 20, 21, *21*, 22
Marin, German, 12
Mars Attacks! (movie), 50

Mexican Air Force, 12
movies, *13*, 50–51, *50–51*
MTE (missing time experience), 9,
    30–31

newspapers, 18, *20*, 21, 44, 45,
    53, 55

Ohio State University, 36, *37*, 39
The Outer Limits (television show),
    33

photographs, 11, *11*, 16
Portsmouth, New Hampshire, 28,
    29
pranks. *See* hoaxes.
Project Blue Book, 26, 45
Project Mogul, 24
psychological problems, 26
psychologists, 14, 28, 31–32, 34

quiz, 54

radio telescopes, 36–37, *36*,
    38–39, 39–40, 41–42, 52–53
researchers. *See* ufologists.
Rome, 44
Roswell Army Air Field, 10, 20,
    20, 22
Roswell, New Mexico, 10, *10*, 12,
    18, *19*, 20–21, 22–23, 24–25

salaries, 55
Saucer-Men (movie), *50*
Sci Fi Channel, 46
SETI (Search for Extra-Terrestrial
    Intelligence), 38, *40*, 41–42,
    41, *42*, 52–53, 55
Shostak, Seth, *40*, 52–53, *52*
Simon, Benjamin, 31, 32
skeptics, 16, 33, 34
sleep paralysis, 34
sociologists, 14
Star Trek television series, 46
Star Wars films, 46
Strange Invaders (movie), 51

Tarter, Jill, *40*

test dummies, 24, *25*
The Man from Planet X (movie), *50*
A Trip to the Moon (movie), 50

UFO Day, 13
ufologists, 9, 14, 22, 26, 44
UFOs, 9, 10, *10*, 11, *11*, 12, *12*,
    13, *13*, 16, 18, 20, 21, 23,
    26, 28–29, 30, 33, 44, *45*
uranium-238, 49

Voyager spacecraft, 48–49, *48–49*

Walters, Edward, 11
War of the Worlds (movie), *51*
Web sites, 55
"Wow!" signal, 36–37, 38,
    39–40, 41
Wright-Patterson Air Force Base,
    23, *23*, 26

Author's Note

If you're interested in learning more about aliens, you may feel like an astronomer who is faced with a huge universe filled with billions of stars. How can you possibly decide where to start? Here are a few ideas:

Surf the Internet. There are hundreds of sites about UFOs and aliens. See the Resources section on pages 56–58 for a list of Web sites that will get you started. But remember that *anyone* can create a Web site. They don't have to be scientists, experts, or even know what they're talking about. How can you figure out which Web sites have good information?

First, take a look at sites that are run by universities or professional organizations, like the Planetary Society or an astronomical society. They will have the most serious and scientific research. Check out their links to other sites. A link is a sign that the experts at one site have looked at other sites and think that they have good information.

Second, read the stories and articles on each site with a critical eye. Some sites have lots of scary UFO stories, but there aren't any details about how the sightings were investigated. The stories may be fun, but you won't get any evidence that will help you decide whether you should believe them.

Find people to talk to. If you're interested in the science of searching for aliens, look for an astronomical society in your area. If you're more interested in getting out in the field and investigating UFO sightings, find a group of people who do this in their spare time. You may find a group of ufologists in your area by doing Internet research, or you may find them just by asking around.

Be persistent. Remember, people have been searching for aliens for a very long time—but *no one* has been able to prove that he or she had contact with an extraterrestrial! I admire people who have the determination to keep trying to answer an important question, even when years go by with no clear result. Follow their example as you start to learn more about this topic, and don't give up until you find out what you want to know!

ACKNOWLEDGMENTS

I would like to thank the following people for their help with this book:

Dr. Amir Alexander
Budd Hopkins
Karen Randall
Dr. Seth Shostak

CONTENT ADVISER: Jerome Clark, Center for UFO Studies